Sue Patrick's

# Workbox System

User's Guide

## Sue Patrick

Wend Publishing
Wake Forest, North Carolina

ISBN: 978-0-9818968-4-7

Published by

Wend Publishing
P.O. Box 233
Wake Forest, NC 27588

Printed in the United States of America

Sue Patrick's Workbox System
User's Guide

Please register your purchase at

**www.workboxsystem.com**

by selecting "Book Registration."

This registration will give you access to
the forms mentioned in this book.

Reference Code:  RA2097

This code is valid for the original
purchaser only.

# My appreciation...

*To God, who has always known I would not willingly take the paths I have been on, but has sent a Counselor and Teacher for me so that I would not be alone.*

*To my husband, Dale.  I wish I were wise enough to always put you first.  I am thankful you are patient with me and allow me to be the obsession-chaser I am.  You are the perfect leader and example.*

*To my children, Jake and Katie.  God gave you both to me and I will be forever thankful. It was only through you that I could truly understand His love.*

*To Joyce, your support, prayers, friendship and  help are precious to me.*

# How to Use this Book

You are either a manual reader or you aren't. I realize that by being a manual reader, I am nearly alone. I read manuals, cover to cover, for everything—even the battery recharger I recently bought.

I recognize that you are probably not a manual reader. That's why this is called a "User's Guide." Perhaps the title will encourage your reading it from cover to cover. However, if that is not the case, please be sure to read **Chapter 4** in order to have a good foundation on the Workbox System. I have many small details in place because they work. I like to think that I am an efficiency seeker and I do not like to do things that are not necessary. I have put the information in **Chapter 4** that is necessary. The other chapters in this book may stand alone and will allow you to pick and choose as you are in need.

If you have questions beyond what this book will provide, please register your purchase with me at: **www.workboxsystem.com**. When you register, you will receive a password which will allow you access to all the sample forms noted in

this book with the  symbol.

# Contents

＄ＶＧ
# Contents

## *The Beginning of the Workbox System*

I am Sue Patrick, a homeschool mom, with a Bachelor's Degree from North Carolina State University. While in the process of pursuing a Master's Degree from NCSU, my oldest child was diagnosed with Autism at the age of two. His diagnosis was a crushing blow to my husband and me, and I found myself caught between two worlds. One in which I was grieving the loss of the child I had hoped for and prayed about for 10 years. And another world in which I was determined to do everything humanly possible to help this child, whom suddenly I didn't think I knew.

I had been completely consumed with the world of infertility and adoption. When our son arrived, he was truly bigger than life and everything we had ever wanted. As I watched him develop over the first 15 months, not only did I not realize, as a first time mother, that he had a severe disability, I only saw that he was incredibly gifted and talented. My hopes, prayers and perceived future for him were unlimited. He was the perfect and beautiful child I had always wanted. But when he was diagnosed, I realized that all those prayers and ideas of who he would become and what would be his future, were crushed. I had to re-order my prayers and hopes for a complete unknown. No one could tell me what my son could achieve, if he would ever talk, interact or learn anything, much less academics.

I did not stay in the world of grief for very long. Instincts for survival and hopes for my son took over. His progress became the most important thing in my life. My priorities were not balanced, and neither God or my husband came first. I do not remember much about my daughter's first year (she was born just as my son was going through the process of diagnosis).

Initially I spent all day raising two small children as best I could, and most of the night researching and making materials and curriculum to help my son grow and develop to his greatest potential. Over the next 10 years, I pursued my son's improvement, balance in my life, and an understanding of homeschooling a special needs child. It was during this time that I developed the Workbox System.

The Workbox System was loosely based on the structured teaching approach from Division TEACCH, Treatment and Education of Autistic and related Communication-handicapped Children, A Division of the UNC Department of Psychiatry. So many of us who were thrown into the world of autism were also thrown into a world of "unnatural" teaching. There are so many people, organizations, institutions, and "professionals" out there who have found the new key to "curing" autism. I learned very quickly that there is no cure for autism, and fortunately, I learned from TEACCH the value of teaching in a structured way to the individual mind. Though TEACCH vehemently stated that there is no cure for autism, I contend that they saved my child's life. They introduced a thought process to me that allowed me to develop this Workbox System[sm]. Without TEACCH and this system, I would not want to imagine where my son would be now.

> *"This system works very well with all homeschools and all children ranging from "typical" to disabled."*

I had such great success with his progress, that I began showing other families with children with developmental disabilities what I had learned, and what was working so very well for my son. Over time, with trial and error, always seeking to understand and improve a system I was developing, I was able to share with more and more families.

My son, who was never considered high functioning, began to function at a very high level—even though he has a language disability that seems insurmountable. Through this system, he has learned so well that he is academically on grade level with his peers.  He participates in groups and social activities, and on sports teams, independently, with his  peers.  I believe this is all due to what I have been able to glean from all existing therapies, theories, and educational plans and to implement them as a home program.  After attending seminars, conferences, and certification programs for nearly every therapy based work for special needs children,  I did not adopt any existing program or other therapies because I thought a meshing of the best of all programs, along with a Specialized Parent-Based approach was the only logical choice.  I am thankful to God every day for giving me that discernment.

Over the years I have shown an uncounted number of families how to successfully work at home to create their best homeschool.  I have worked with parents whose children range from "too wiggly" to severely disabled to just plain large numbers of children in their home, and have found that I simply did not have enough time to reach as many people as would call me for help.

I have now packaged my system, Sue Patrick's

Workbox System$^{SM}$ in an effort to reach even more families working to achieve the highest academic and cognitive potential they can in their own children. This system works very well with all homeschools and all children ranging from "typical" to disabled.

ᘒᔕᘕ
# Chapter 1

## *The Benefits of Homeschooling*

Homeschooling benefits run into infinity. I could make a very long list and argue forever on which items should be at the top. The bottom line is that we only have our children (usually) at home for 18 years. They are only under foot for about 9 years. There will never be enough time to spend with our children before they are adults and raising children of their own. Time spent loving, growing, nurturing, guiding, teaching, preparing and disciplining our children should only be treasured. While our children should not be the center of our universe, they are one of our greatest blessings.

Beyond the emotional and philosophical reasons above, for those of you who are a bit more concrete, I will try to develop a very real and practical list of homeschooling benefits.

**Family.** I believe family is becoming a lost entity in America. Do we not all marvel at other countries and cultures who are unselfish enough to make family the priority? Unselfish because it takes time, money and effort above and beyond the American daily grind to make family and extended family a priority. Who wants to make the effort for their mother-in-law to live with them, or for the "between jobs" brother? That has possibly translated into some other selfish attitudes such as "What about my career?" "What about time for **me**?" I have yet to be able to find answers to or support for these questions in the Bible.

> *"Homeschooling can be the ultimate family opportunity. It is what your family makes of it."*

Homeschooling creates a family relationship that is very hard to achieve within the framework of public or private schools, tutoring, lessons, sports, appointments, and carpooling to no less than 100 different "opportunities." Homeschooling can be the ultimate family opportunity. It is what your family makes of it. Homeschool families may still be going in way too many directions, but at least they can benefit from 6 to 8 hours per day that other families must commit to be apart and in separate schools. That makes for 180 days x 8 hours per day, or 1,440 hours per year, that homeschoolers are growing together in a family relationship.

**Character.** You are your child's ultimate peer.

Their siblings are also their peers.  It is not that they are not subject to the opinions, behaviors and influences of others, but you are able to be in direct conversations with them as they begin to interpret the world around them.  When they are fully secure and rooted in your family's values, they will be more capable of handling the unstructured world of public education—in college.  There is no need to tackle it all before then.  Their development will not be stunted.  They will still be able to think for themselves.  Who doesn't want their children to hang with the "right" crowd?  That right crowd is your family.

**Education**.  There is no doubt in my mind that education is more meaningful, richer, fuller, deeper, broader and far more nurturing when done by a loving, discerning parent. No teacher could ever care about your child as much as you do.  No teacher, year to year, could ever understand the educational needs of your child as you do.  You do not need to start at square one on day one of each new school year.  We always know our children and our school year never ends.   A homeschooler finds a way to educate with more depth, no matter what they are doing.  When you homeschool, a trip through the car wash, a wait behind the garbage truck and a visit to the dentist are continuous teaching moments.  We teach by asking questions—not always by opening a text book and expecting a 2nd grader to learn from it.

**Faith**. I have listed faith last, but for many of us it is first. I simply cannot understand teaching without God in the classroom. There is no other basis for history, science, geography, math or any subject on earth, than to start with God. It is popular for public schools to have a behavior and discipline "control plan" based on character. It is nothing but hollow without the Bible for its foundation. Man simply cannot be "good" and "reasonable" on his own, so why waste time trying to teach small children in public school to do just that?

**If I am already committed to homeschooling, why should I put in the extra work of a Specialized Education Plan?**

Simply by virtue of homeschooling we are already providing a Specialized Education Plan for our children. There are thousands of families out there who are homeschooling with "boxed" curriculum and reading, "Teacher says ..." straight from the teacher manual. That is certainly a huge step up from public school, but we can do better than that. We can make school fun and interesting both for us as teachers and for our children as students. School should be and can be fun!

ꙮ

# Chapter 2

## *How We Teach and Train*

Families choose, and are sometimes forced to choose, homeschooling for many different reasons.  Some homeschools exist for years without formally knowing why.  They have some notion, but no written plan, statement or philosophy for the accomplishments of their homeschool.  They also have no formal written plan, statement or philosophy for what their children will learn, what they want their children to learn, or how they want to mold their children's minds, character or life paths.  While the thought of figuring this out for your family and writing it down may seem too overwhelming (which is why you have never tackled it before), I would challenge you to simply take out a legal pad for each child and start jotting down what you feel would be important for your child to learn over the next three months.  Even if you never put together a formal plan, the next three months will have more direction.

While there are as many styles of homeschools as there are actual homeschools, I believe every school can  "lighten up and have fun" while at the same time deepening their children's understanding of all subject matter. It does not take supreme creativity, as so many moms believe. I have no natural creativity whatsoever, had never considered myself teacher material, nor was I particularly organized. But somehow, when I put the right system together, I created an environment in which I could more clearly understand the needs of my children's education. I could more clearly understand their most effective ways of learning. Once I looked at those input channels in a logical and sequential way, I was able to see how to teach and provide curriculum in a way that made sense to my children. I'm not creative, I am logical. Logic can look like creativity at times. So believe it or not, logical, creative homeschooling is fun, effective, efficient—and possible for everyone.

When your homeschool is logical and creative—meaning your children are learning in a way (individually) that makes sense to them, school is effective and fun. When your homeschool is fun, the whole day is self perpetuating. You love to homeschool, the kids love, or at least like, to learn. The school hours go by quickly and no one feels that school is what we do until we can do something better. School is what we do! And fun is what we have while we are doing school.

There are two comments that I continually receive from people who use my Workbox System^sm. The first is generally, "This has changed our lives forever!" The second is, "I cannot believe how much work we get done and in so much less time." Each time I hear these comments from exuberant new Workbox System users, I smile gratefully and nod and tell them how happy I am that this is working so well for them. The truth is, everyone says the same thing and I am no longer amazed by it. But my smile and returned exuberance is real, because I am so very grateful that they were willing to try and were able to look past their traditional ideas of what school should look like and what children should be able to do on their own.

> *"Learning how to learn is one of the most important things we can teach our children."*

I believe it is **our** job to train up our children. Our children should become smart, sequential, forward thinking, self-driven, independent people. But I don't think they typically have to achieve it by themselves. Some of our children will never blossom into the individual who "loves to learn." But at least they will have learned **how** to learn. Learning how to learn is one of the most important things we can teach our children. It is a first step many parents just assume that kids will have accomplished on their own.    Some of them have not. We must start by giving our children their learning materials in a way that will make sense to them, so that they can learn.  If we do it any other way, learning will be too hard and it will never be fun—nor will our job of training them be easy.

༄

# Chapter 3

## *What is the Workbox System?*

This book will teach you how to organize and structure your homeschool in a way that optimizes time, space, effort, planning and independence.  With this system, you and your children will move through your homeschool day more efficiently and with greater understanding than ever before.  The way you teach will be fun for your children and more rewarding for you.  You will be able to spend more time having fun with your children and less time on the "business" side of homeschooling. Once you have this system in place, you will truly wonder how you ever homeschooled without it.

The Workbox System consists of two components:

    1.  The Physical Structure of the System
    2.  The Educational Philosophy

### *The Physical Structure*
The structure of the Workbox System simply consists of a rack or shelves for each child filled with Workboxes, numbering for the Workboxes, and a

special **Schedule Strip*** to help guide them through their day. The Workboxes hold your child's school work for the entire day. When your child comes to school in the morning, he or she can see all their Workboxes filled with the day's work. They know that when they complete all the Workboxes, they are done for the day. Continually throughout the day, they can see how much work there is to do and what it will mean to be finished. They can see the hard work ahead, and they can see the fun things to come. By including difficult work, fun work, projects, centers and group activities, most children will actually look forward to coming to school in the morning.

## *The Educational Philosophy*

The philosophy of the Workbox System is to provide:

1. Structure
2. A firm foundation in discipline
3. A clear and visual presentation of their curriculum
4. A way to present expectations for their curriculum in a clear and logical way
5. Fun and interesting materials
6. Important educational repetition
7. An expectation of greater independence

*See Chapter 4

The structure provided by the Workbox System goes deeper than just the physical setup. This structure provides both teacher and student an air of organization, clear expectations, and even a level of peace and calm, all of which creates a better learning environment. Because the expectations are so visual and so obvious, the discipline of sticking with their work through completion is easily achieved. It is much easier for the  homeschool parent to prepare for school, which makes it easier for a more consistent school year from day to day, week to week and month to month. You will find yourself missing almost no school days with this system and needing far fewer "teacher workdays." The structure will be every bit as much for your benefit as for your child's.

> *"Seeing what work there is to do, what is expected of him, and what it will mean to be finished for the day will have a very positive influence."*

Because the child's work is in clear and separate Workboxes, he will always be able to see how much work is left for the day as well as be able to see the enjoyable activities he is looking forward to. Seeing  what work there is to do, what is expected of him, and what it will mean to be finished for the day, will have a very positive influence.

I will show you how to incorporate interesting and enticing materials and curriculum, so that the benefits of being able to see their work all day long will be optimized.  When he can see a few Workboxes down the row that there is something really fun to do, he will be more motivated to get through the tougher materials that are not his favorite.

Repetition is an important aspect of education. Through activities targeting repetition, so often the children won't even feel like they are in school. These activities will feel like a school break for them.

Finally, the natural motivation that is created with the flow of the Workbox System, paired with some discipline tips, will create a greater amount of independence in your child.  Children who have never wanted to work on their own without "Mom" sitting there will now happily work  independently and feel proud of  themselves for doing so.

ᔕᵛᒐ
# Chapter 4

## *Sue Patrick's Workbox System*[sm]

### *Who is this system for?*

Who is this system aimed at? What children will learn best with this system? The answer to the first question is You. No matter who you are, it is aimed at you and will work for you. The children that it works best with is all children. It doesn't matter if they are self-starters, kinesthetic, ADHD, creative, artistic, visual, auditory, learning disabled, developmentally disabled, or last, but not least, a High Schooler! In fact, I started both of my children on my system at 18 months old, and I have converted many a High School homeschooler to it successfully. Many homeschoolers with teenagers have balked at the system feeling it was "too immature" before actually using the Workbox System. Teenagers probably need the structure to help them organize for the in-depth learning they require more than 3 year olds do. It will keep your teenager on track and keep your toddler busy "doing school" while your whole family can learn together.

## *The Makeup of the Workbox System*

There are two main components of the Workbox System[sm]. The first is the physical structure of the system and the second is the educational philosophy of how to present the child's work. This philosophy incorporates review and assessments, and is interesting and fun. Sound like the perfect educational plan? It is. And it is so easy that you can begin simply and immediately. I have given my workshop to many people who have told me that they stopped at Wal-Mart or Target on the way home in order to get the physical structure in place for the next day. People have understood the system and its potential benefits immediately and were motivated to begin **tomorrow**. It's not rocket science, it just makes sense.

## *The Physical Structure*

The physical structure involves very simple materials:

> *A wire shoe rack
> *Between 6 and 15 clear shoe boxes
> *Numbered cards with schedule strip
> *Velcro
> *Structured schedule cards (for activities and centers)
> *A correctly sized desk with correctly sized chair
> *Other optional supplies which will be outlined later

As shown in the above photo, the wire rack is placed to the left of the child's desk, and Workboxes are filled with the day's curriculum.  Each individual Workbox on the wire rack has it's own subject or work in it.

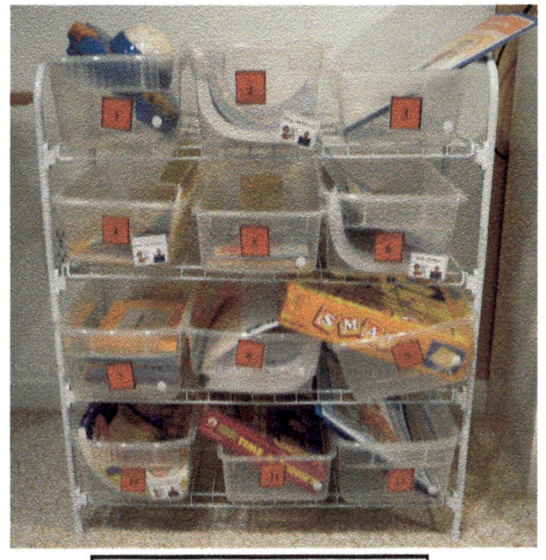

The Workboxes on the wire rack with the numbers placed on the end.

The schedule strip placed on their desk to directs them to each Workbox or to centers.

The Workboxes are numbered and the schedule strip is loaded with the schedule of work for the day.  This schedule of work will include regular curriculum, review, and centers, which will be covered later.  Another important feature is that individual Workboxes are labeled with a "Work with Mom" card if it is a one-on-one teaching Workbox. Your child will always understand which Workboxes are to be worked independently and which Workboxes you will be teaching or helping him with.

This physical set-up will allow your children to see all the work that is to be done, how to do it, when to be independent and when to call you over to help.  At any point of the day whether it is the first minute they are in school or two hours into their school day,  they will know how much work is left to be done and what it will mean to be finished.



It is very motivating to see all their work at all times, as well as see it disappear as the day goes on.

## *The Process*

The process of the system proceeds as follows:

Placed on the child's desk is a schedule strip.

This strip has a number card corresponding to each Workbox.  Interspersed on the schedule strip and among the numbered Workbox cards are centers and any other events or interruptions to the school day. They may include snacks, break, musical instrument practice, P.E. activities, chores and so on.  I would encourage people to plan for school being school and for other activities to be left for before school (such as chores) or after school (such as professional music lessons and outside group activities).  That way, the priority and attitude is set that school is important and comes first.  I also encourage a lot of variety, hands-on materials, experiments, centers, and group time. This variety actually helps add to their independence and focus, as well as a great enjoyment of their school day.

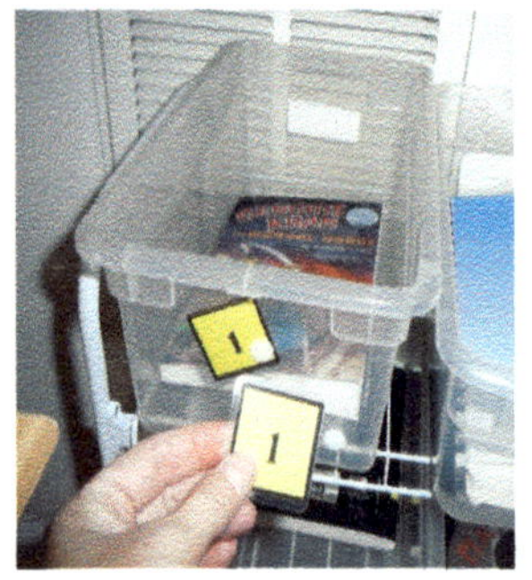 

Matching the schedule strip numbers to the
Workboxes.

As they sit down at their desk, they remove the first card from their schedule strip (the number "1" card) and match it to the number 1 on the first Workbox (attach the number to the Workbox with Velcro). They pick that Workbox up and place it in front of them on their desk. They re-move all the work from that Workbox. Everything in that Workbox makes the work to be done self-evident, easy to determine when they are "finished" and includes all the materials they need to do the work. No time should be spent trying to figure "what" to do or to be looking



Yellow sticky letting them know what work is to be done.

for materials (pencil, Bible, dictionary, protractor…). Everything is either in the Workbox or within arm's reach. Each child has a shelf nearby that holds a Bible, dictionary, calculator or any needed reference materials. The child then does the work that is in that Workbox and places everything back in the Workbox. The completed Workbox is then placed on the floor to their right. Some children will benefit from a tough tote on the floor to their right to hold all the finished Workboxes (this is simply a way of adding more structure and organization).

This tough tote to the right of her desk collects the finished Workboxes. Not all children need this, but it does provide more structure.

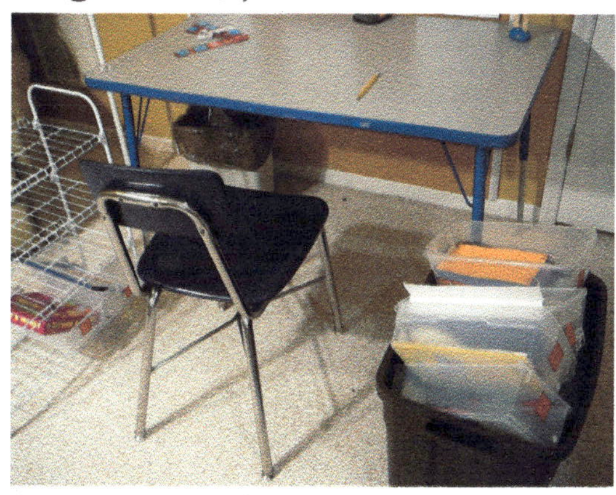

The child then goes on to the next item on their schedule strip. This could be a "center" card, a group time or circle time card, or simply the Workbox 2 card. They work their way  through the Workboxes one by one, removing the Workbox, doing the work, placing everything back in it and placing the Workbox in the finished pile (or tough tote). This way, the wire rack with their work is continuing to empty and they are visually motivated to keep moving in order to complete their day.

Having schedule cards interspersed between Workbox numbers will allow them to move around to other educational activities, centers, and group time between their regular work. This adds a good variety, breaks up monotony, allows for interaction between children, and can actually make them feel like they are getting a break when they're really doing even more work. These alternative education opportunities such as centers will allow you to add more repetition or a way of teaching the same subject or material in a different way to ensure they are really learning.

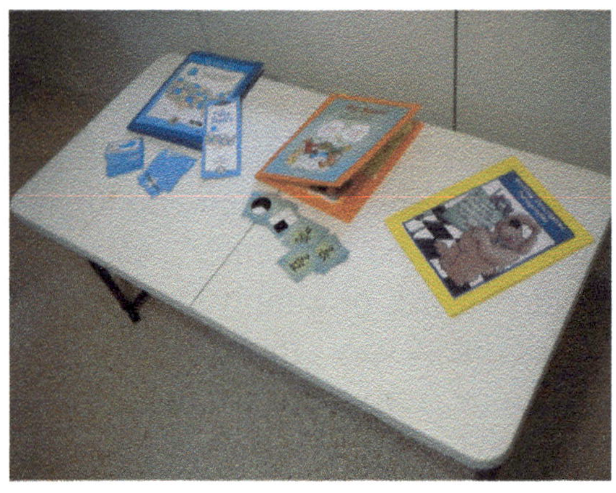

Example of a "Centers" table in which the child can pick two of three centers to do.

**Poster Centers**
Posters are made interactive by buying two
and cutting up the duplicate making
interactive pieces attach with Velcro.

A Centers Table

Science Center

# Independence

Many homeschoolers are plagued with independence issues. Children become comfortably addicted to having mom sit next them. Along with the need for mom to sit next to them, comes the need to talk. I find that there is way too much talking going on in homeschools. Homeschool children often develop the skill of speaking out-loud every thought that enters their mind, whenever it enters it! These two issues can seem innocent and necessary with a pre-schooler, but quite aggravating and unproductive well into elementary and middle school. And the unnecessary talking by middle school can tend to be unproductive prompting and arguing by the parent.

I have developed two small, but very effective tools for correcting both these issues. Most children will be cured of the need for mom and too much talking within the first few days of using these tools. But it will take commitment and consistency on your part.

Tool 1: An "I need help" card.

The child should be given a few of these cards each day.  Usually 3 or 4 will do.  Place a small strip of Velcro on the left side of their desk with these cards on it in the morning.

If the child feels he needs help with a particular Workbox, but it does not have a "Work with Mom" card on it, then he may quietly get your attention and ask for help.  Your job is to make those help cards seem very, very valuable.  "Are you sure you need help with this Workbox?" "I'll be happy to help you, but you'll need to give me one of your help cards. That will only leave you with two more…"  Often he will change his mind, not wanting to use up a help card he may need later.  But if he still wants the help, do help him happily, and make a ceremony out of his handing over the card.  Most children will truly be over needing your extra help by the end of the week.

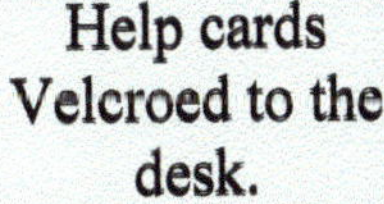

Help cards Velcroed to the desk.

Tool 2:  "I'm ready to work!" card.

Many children will benefit from, and enjoy, having reminder cards on their desk.  I make them a little more fun and interesting by placing them on craft sticks and inserting them in a lump of clay. In this picture it is the "I'm ready to work!" card and "Wait" card, but there may be other needs this works well for.  A restroom break card, a quiet, please card,  a question card and so on.

Non-verbal reminder cards. These are reminding them to get back to work, or to wait for mom.

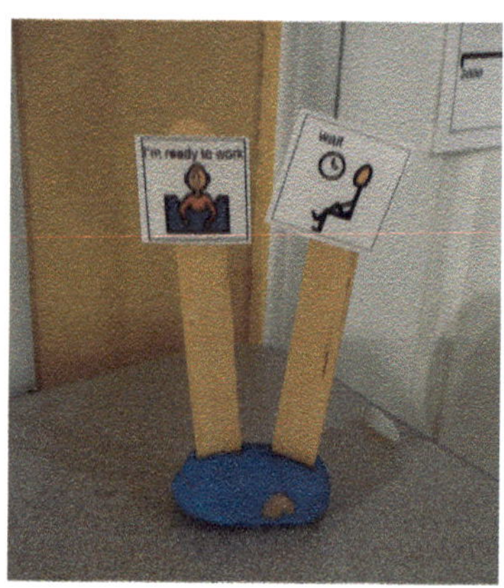

All this is to help quiet the classroom so there are less distractions and interruptions. The picture card is a constant, non-verbal reminder in front of them. If need be, you can simply and quietly point to the card to get them back on task. If the child is staring out into space, get his attention and point to the "ready to work" card. If he is talking when he shouldn't, point to the "quiet please" card.

After a week of using the appropriate cards consistenly and squelching your natural bent toward talking too much, everyone can be better trained and better focused.

ↂ♡ↁ

## *Chapter 5*

### *How a Day Works*

It is very beneficial for children to have a routine in which your expectations are clear and also includes plenty of visual reminders.  An example of a typical school day may include personal care, chores, practicing musical instruments, *running* (I'll touch on this later), and of course, school work.  Having a set routine and a set time for the school day routine are a first step to structured success.

Starting their day with a schedule and clear expectations will keep the children in the right frame of mind (productive and working) to move them through the school day. Below are sample schedules to start their day.

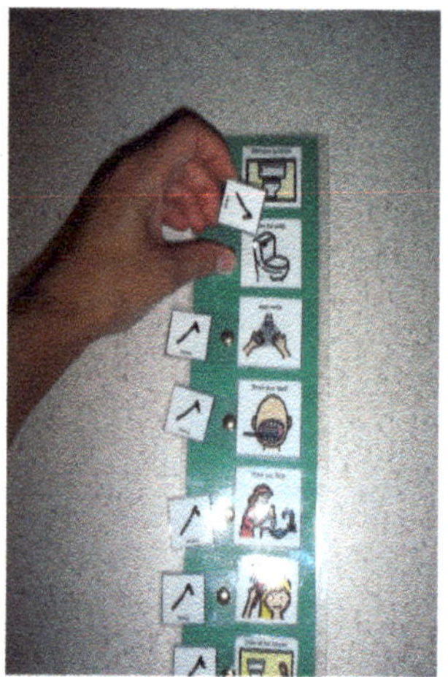
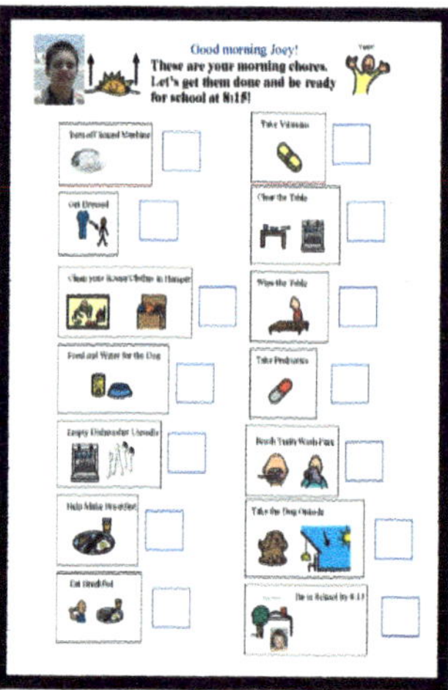

In this case, the child will move through his morning schedule and be ready for school at 8:15.

At the completion of the morning schedule, he is given a special card that he puts in a "school" pocket. This way, he mentally "clocks in" to school. It sets a visual frame of reference that we are in school and ready to work. Most children (even those older than you would think) really enjoy this card and checking in. They will also enjoy moving that card to the finished pocket when they leave school. This is a small step, but actually has a strong effect.

This child is "clocking out" into the finished pocket at the end of the school day.

After the child has clocked into school, he will move to his desk. I always say that this is the most quiet time of the day. Children are happy to get to the classroom to look over everything.

They will check out all the Workboxes to see what they are doing that day, and eagerly scan the room to see what centers and projects to look forward to. The extra centers and projects are great motivators for the entire school day.

Next, the child will use his schedule strip to start work. Alternatively, you may want to start your school day with a group time for all the children. This could be for devotion, sharing, common subjects and curriculum, or (my favorite) board games, as well as many other "together" options.

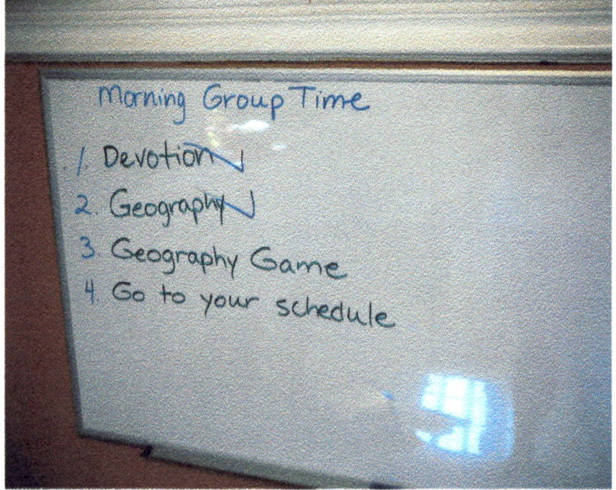


Group time schedule. Check off the items as they are done. When completed, they all go back to their desks and schedule strips.

If you do choose to start with group time, I think it's a good idea to have a list or schedule of what that time will entail to help keep them interested and able to attend.  The more information the children have as to what is expected of them and how long they will be doing a given task, the better the focus and behavior.  Simply writing on a white board the list of things being covered in a group time will keep them focused and participating.

As your child starts working at his desk, he will take the current Workbox off the cart and place it in front of him on his desk. Everything he needs to complete the work in that Workbox is to be   included inside the Workbox—even the pencil.  When he pulls the work out of the Workbox, it must also be visually clear what he is to do.   Generally a yellow sticky note will do the trick.  For example, **Read pages 22-36** or **Do Problems 1-29.**  Virtually any curriculum or textbook will fit into the Workboxes.  For the very few items that will not fit, place a yellow sticky note in the box indicating what is to be done and place the too large materials underneath his desk.  He can retrieve them when it is time for that Workbox.

For Workboxes that are not independent, there needs to be an indication that you will work with him.  I like to make up "Work with Mom" cards and place those outside the Workbox on those particular Workboxes. That way, if there is not a "Work with Mom" card, he knows he is to work **independently** on that box.

After completing the Workbox, he places all the materials back into the Workbox and either places the finished Workbox on the floor to the right or in a tough tote to the right.

It is important to remove the Workboxes in this way so that the cart with the work continues to visually motivate him as his work disappears. I cannot emphasize this effect enough—that as their work is disappearing, they are more motivated to keep moving and finish their work for the day. If children simply put those Workboxes back onto the cart, they will not benefit nearly as much.

This child is nearly finished, easily recognizes it and is eager to keep moving.

It is very helpful to alternate the materials you place in the Workbox with more challenging materials preceding easier or more desired subjects. If your child is quite challenged by math, be sure to put a more favored activity in the Workbox following math. His being able to see the fun activity coming up will be another motivator to get through the math. That fun activity is still school, still curriculum and still a productive part of their school day, but it will be helpful if it is a fun, hands-on type of activity.

The child will continue working through the Workboxes via the schedule strip and moving from activities to Workboxes. Nearly 100% of my clients tell me that they cannot believe how fast the school day goes and that they are able to get twice as much work done in half the time. I love hearing the astonished reports from families, but I am never surprised. This system is very motivating for the children to get their work done without dawdling and it is also so easy to pick up right where you left off if ever you are interrupted. By the same token, as you jump between different children, it will be very easy for you to tell what you need to do with that child without feeling the struggle of getting acclimated to

> *"Nearly 100% of my clients tell me that they cannot believe how fast the school day goes and that they are able to get twice as much work done in half the time."*

child #2 after having just worked with child #1.

Everything is visually obvious. It is also very easy to gather everyone together at any time for group projects and when they are finished, everyone goes back to their Workbox System and is instantly able to see where they left off and to get right back to work. Before everyone knows it, the school day is finished and they get to "clock out" for the day.

### *Juggling multiple children*

I am often asked about problems with children finishing their Workboxes at different times. They will finish at different times. This can also be a motivator. When one child clocks out of school at 11:30 and the other one still has 5 boxes to work through, he'll be even more motivated to keep moving. Most likely the next day, that child will have worked through those Workboxes more effectively.

There can also be a concern of two children moving to a "Work with Mom" Workbox at the same time. The way to approach this is to work with the less flexible child according to his schedule. Ask the other child or children to move onto the next item on the schedule strip, knowing that when you are free, you both will go back to the "Work with Mom" Workbox. That child will still easily be able to stop what he is doing, go to that Workbox with you, and then know exactly where to jump back in when you are through. Another option, especially for young children, is to have a "wait" center. This may be either a specially cordoned off area with special educational toys that are not normally played with, or it may simply be a separate table with a puzzle, K'nex or special project. It shouldn't be so involved that they won't want to leave it once you are free to work with them. But it should be involved enough that they won't feel slighted when you are busy with another child.

### *A sample day*

This is an example of a common school day. This flow has worked well for me for years, and even the most loosely organized clients of mine have been able to convert to a very structured day. This sample includes only school-aged children, but preschoolers will fit into this schedule nicely. A section on preschoolers is included in Chapter 11. I cannot emphasize enough, the importance of your discipline and consistency when beginning this program. While your day may look very different from this example, you must finish what you begin, and follow the "rules" of the system as I have outlined.  I have spent 11 years changing and fine tuning, problem solving and improving the smallest of details.  I have worked with such a cross-section of families, that I know what works.  There really are specific reasons for the rules and methods I have in place.  After following my rec-ommendations and rules, and having trained your children on the Workbox System, you will then be able to make changes beneficial to your family and homeschool.  But I greatly encourage you to use the system as outlined before making changes on your own.

You may register your purchase using the form in the front of this book.  After register-ing, you will receive a password allowing you access to the forms referenced in this book. 

**Children awake by 7:00 am**

**Chores & Breakfast by 8:30 am**
Using a schedule, they immediately work through their morning of self care, individual chores, and breakfast.  (In our home, we see no reason for television or other distractions in the morning.)

**School from 8:30 to 12:30 pm**
After breakfast, they are handed their "clock in" picture and they immediately place it in the
appropriate pocket and head for school. I find that most children up through grade 6 can be finished with school in this time if you are schooling 5 days a week. Using the Workbox System will allow for much more to be accomplished in a short period of time.

**Lunch and Free Time 12:30-2:30 pm**
I like to plan ahead for lunch, keep it simple and hopefully have the children involved in the preparation and responsibility. After a busy morning of chores and school, most children are happy to find something appropriate to do on their own.

**Run on the Treadmill 2:30-3:30**
Getting your children on a running program is so very beneficial. For the families that I have been able to convince to do this, no one has ever regretted the investment. I suggest a treadmill because I have yet to see families be able to have any consistency solely running outside. There are so many benefits to running every day: discipline, perseverance, commitment, neurological development, physical fitness...and the list goes on forever. My children started running on the treadmill at age 5 and quickly built up to 3 miles per day. At this point they have done it for 8 years with no injuries or problems—

only benefits. Please refer to my website for sample running schedules. These schedules will allow you to build your child's stamina and running abilities. Some children may seem to be very "awkward" runners at the start. But over time, their bodies will find more efficient running mechanics.

### Quiet Time 3:30-4:15

If you are a Christian, this again will be beneficial in countless ways. It will set a firm foundation for the importance of prayer, Bible reading and quiet time. If you are not a Christian, it will still give you and your home a chance to re-set for the remainder of the day and let everyone begin anew refreshed. I think it's important for all of us to spend time alone. It's yet another opportunity to develop self discipline.

### Play and Free Time 4:15-6:00

If your children are able to appropriately handle free time on their own, this is the time for it. If not, I would further structure their day with schedules and supervised play (see preschool section). This way you can finally get to the laundry and all the chores you need to do.

### Dinner and Family Time 6:00-8:00

The day is over before we know it! Having very small children and older children may or may not alter this sample schedule. But ultimately, I believe a family runs better when they are organized and purposeful.

### *When do I prepare for school?*

Good question. The answer is different for every household. It depends on your sleep habits, the curriculum you use, the number of children and ages, your personality, and most importantly: your level of commitment. That sounds harsh, but committing to homeschooling and all the work it entails is very serious. It seems to me that people often pick their methods and their curriculum based on how little work it will entail. Homeschooling is hard work and it's a serious job. Homeschooling is not what we do when we don't have anything else to do. It's not what we do when we're not doing laundry and cooking and cleaning.

*Homeschooling is what we do first.* In order to raise a generation of homeschooled children that are good representatives of what it means to homeschool, we must be committed. It is mission work and it is a full time job. Having it take any less position in your life will be to short change your children and yourself. You have been called to homeschool for a reason, and to do it well and to the best of your ability.

❧❧❧

# Chapter 6

## *Curriculum and Materials*

A school day may consist of a more classic school curriculum (Abeka) or a unit study (like Konos, Five in a Row, or one you have written yourself), a mish mash of curriculum you have put together yourself, or even toys and games. The Workbox System works with anyone's curriculum and work load. The important thing is that their school day has variety, review, new materials and fun. All this can be achieved with 12 small Workboxes!

> *"Our goal should not be to simply get through the material."*

The workboxes help you to create natural breaks, a more sensible simplification of their materials, and added review as with file folders and centers. By mixing up the day's schoolwork in the Workboxes, you can create more independence, greater concrete learning and an education that will actually stick rather than "going in one ear and out the other." Our goal should not be to simply get through the material. We are building our childrens' minds year after year, perhaps teaching the same materials though a little differently and more in-depth each year.

A good way to get started incorporating your curriculum and implementing more fun is to list all your child's curriculum on a "Curriculum Grid."

1. List all your subjects/ curriculum on the right hand column along with the number of times per-week you would like to teach that subject.

2. Then disperse the work throughout the grid and use as a guide during the week.

| Monday | Tuesday | Wednesday | Thursday | Friday | Notes/Wknd |
|---|---|---|---|---|---|
| 1. History | 1. Math | 1. | 1. Latin | 1. Math | History x3 Spelling x2 |
| 2. Math | 2. Spelling | 2. History | 2. Spelling | 2. Latin | Math x4 Latin x3 |
| 3. Latin | 3. | 3. | 3. | 3. | (And so on...) |
| 4. | 4. | 4. Math | 4. | 4. | |
| 5. | 5. | 5. | 5. History | 5. | |
| 6. | 6. | 6. | 6. | 6. | |
| 7. | 7. | 7. | 7. | 7. | |
| 8. | 8. | 8. | 8. | 8. | |
| 9. | 9. | 9. | 9. | 9. | |
| 10. | 10. | 10. | 10. | 10. | |
| 11. | 11. | 11. | 11. | 11. | |
| 12. | 12. | 12. | 12. | 12. | |

Curriculum Grid by Workbox System.com

Example of box system grid for helping to fill the boxes each day.

By first listing each piece of curriculum, then listing the number of times per week you would like the child to work on that curriculum, you will already be much more organized and purposeful in your school day. This is a good way to ensure you do not forget any curriculum or subject matter you want to introduce. After listing the actual curriculum, you will then have space on the form for the remaining Workboxes. These are the opportunities for review (quizzes, file folder activities, centers, projects, and art) as well as some more fun (physics and science experiments, unit study-type reading materials, posters and projects). With these added items dispersed throughout the boxes, throughout the day, the child begins to be more motivated for their school day. These other boxes are more fun and the children literally can't wait to get to them.

I suggest you copy the Curriculum Grid onto a different color of paper for each child and slip it into a sheet protector. I like to keep this and the "Log Grid" forms in a 1/2 inch three ring notebook. Each day I pull this notebook out to both fill the Workboxes and also to record what I have put into the Workboxes.

Log Grid to record what you put in their Workboxes day. Each dated box is for one child, per day.

The Log Grid is a simple form for recording their academic day to keep for your records. People often ask me about lesson plans. Lesson plans are primarily a function of your state laws. In my state we have no requirement for lesson plans and I find them to be more of a frustration than a help. I keep curriculum listed on the Curriculum Grid for as long as I am using it. That way I don't forget to include it in our school day. I simply keep progressing at my child's pace until we have achieved from that curriculum what we aimed or until it is finished. I see no point in "planning" lessons with a schedule. We will progress at the pace I feel is appropriate at the time. A lesson plan has the potential to either slow us down or frustrate us if it is too hurried.

## *Review Materials*

It is important to incorporate review into every subject, every day. No one hears everything the first time and no one retains everything. But little bits of review day by day help to cement the material we wish would immediately absorb. Sometimes as adults, we forget how much we know and simply expect our children to know and retain immediately. The material seems so obvious and evident to us, so why don't they know it? They will...with review.

## *Posters...great centers and great review*

You can find posters that cover all subjects and all grade levels.  However, a poster hanging on the wall rarely has real teaching benefit.  It is best to buy two posters, laminate the first one and cut up the individual subject matter pieces of the second. Then laminate those pieces and apply Velcro to make the first poster hands-on and interactive. This is an extremely inexpensive tool with great benefits.  Often you can use these posters for years, especially if you have more children coming up.  They are very easy to store as well.  See Resources for poster display and storage ideas.

Schedule Strip with "poster" center card to direct them to posters in between Workboxes.

You can then make a "center" of posters by hanging 3 or 4 on the wall and keep the interactive matching pieces in a ziplock bag just beneath the poster. When they reach a "poster" card on their schedule, they then go to the poster wall. It is great review material, they get to get out of their seat and it is a lot of fun for them. It's a learning break!

## *File Folder Games*

File Folder games are a fun way to add repetition and specialized teaching into your child's school day. They also provide a way to easily have school on a day you may not have otherwise. For those inevitable days when you are sick or some project has come along that needs your attention, instead of canceling school, you can give your children a day of File Folder activities. It will be fun for them, and more satisfying for you that you were able to have a school day.

File Folder games and activities are a compact set of learning activities done on a pre-made business file folder. They are generally laminated and have an active component to them using Velcro. You may find them free for the printing on the Internet, or you can make them yourself. They are excellent for working on a particular need of your child, or there are many, many books you may purchase from Teacher stores, Amazon or Ebay with the activities already made up and ready to be put together.

File Folder activities can be found for every subject from pre-school through middle school quite easily.  You will have to search harder for high school materials, and of course, making them yourself may be the best option of all.  After making some of the pre-made ones from books, you will get the idea and hang of it.  Below is a picture of one I made for learning the rules, terms, and  names of the court lines of  tennis when my child was taking beginning tennis lessons.  See Resources for File Folder Activity sources.

## *Centers*

Centers may be thought of much like File Folder Games.  They provide repetition, fun, and perhaps a built-in school day.  But centers also provide more opportunity to work on independence, sequencing, logical thinking, self organization and a more in-depth subject review. Also, centers allow the child to feel like they are taking a break during their school day, when they really aren't. Centers are a very important part of my school day that I find well worth the effort. When children come to school in the morning, it is what they look forward to the most. Centers are well worth the effort for the motivation they naturally provide.

Also, like File Folder Activities, Centers may be purchased in book form, made up by you, or simply set up as a separate space from some part of curriculum you already have and do, such as a science center. Simply taking a given subject such as science or geography and setting it up in a special place or a particular table will make it seem like more fun and something to look forward to.

Dressing a table up with eye protection and a special supply kit will make science seem like more of an event. Placing hands-on materials such as a globe and map with map wheel will make a geography center look like something they can't wait to get to. The following are pictures of some Centers I have made:

Science Center

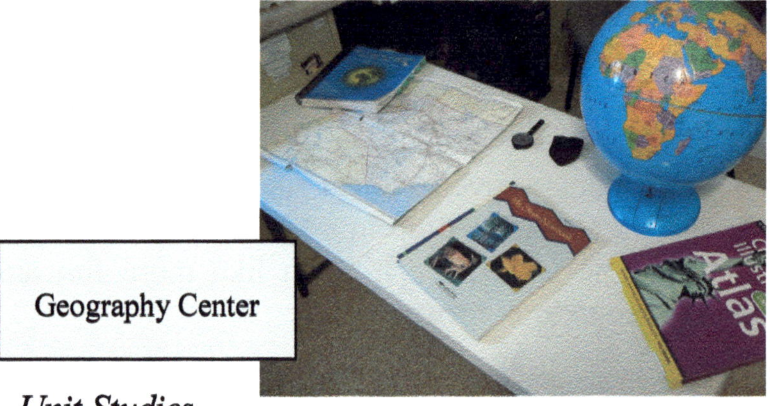



Geography Center

*Unit Studies*

There was a time when I felt that you were either a Unit Study person or you weren't (and I wasn't). I have come to appreciate the value of unit studies and have especially learned that they needn't be all-consuming nor a complete effort and energy drain on your part. Unit Studies create a special "experiential" form of learning that can provide a level and depth of learning that you may not be able to achieve otherwise.  Unit Studies can also help "connect the dots" and pull together some subjects that children might not understand otherwise. For instance, studying the human body might seem too in-depth for young children or may seem like a subject you should take an entire semester to cover with older children.  But with a simple Unit Study, you can quickly cover the entire body, organs and systems and be able to pull it all together in a way the child will understand the big picture in a week for an older child and even a couple days for a young one.

Unit Study
Materials

A Unit Study can also be a good way of covering a subject just once a week for a group or co-op, or perhaps a "Fridays" activity to look forward to in your own homeschool. I often have several Unit Studies going at any given time. I prefer to write my own and use a lot of sources, desktop publishing, hands-on activities and materials, different media and books. They can take as much as a year on an infrequent schedule to complete.

A huge benefit of Unit Studies is that you may bring out those materials every year or every other year. Keep it all organized in a small tote. Each time you re-do the Unit Study, add more depth and projects to it. It will naturally build on their experience and review at the same time. It will be a great way of re-using the time and effort you initially put into it.

## *Quizzes and Tests*

These ever so traditional components of school are still useful, but can be made so much more fun with a few changes. It is also a skill that needs to be developed. Many homeschoolers are at a "testing" disadvantage simply because it is not a natural part of their curriculum.

I have given my children tests from the very beginning. It is not only a measure of what they may have learned, but it also works on logic and sequencing—skills I believe are very important. There are companies that make end of year pre-test books. I was able to give individual sheets from those books throughout the year as both review and for teaching my children how to take tests. Think of them as a sort of textbook.

Tests and Quizzes can also be made into more hands-on forms as well as more interactive than the standard paper and pencil variety. They can be in the form of file folder activities, homemade board games, GeoSafari toys, interactive Microsoft Word documents*, flash cards, and many other forms. I'm sure the Classical educator will disagree with testing in the early years, but the simple fact is that testing will always be an expected way of presenting what a child has "learned." We may as well teach them the skill of testing along with so many other life skills.

## *Additional Curriculum and Books*

I cannot imagine having homeschooled in any other era than now. We have so many resources and technologies available to give our children the benefit of learning the same subject from many different sources. The more ways a subject is presented, the

*See the resources section

greater the depth of understanding a child can achieve. For example, I like to use Math-U-See for teaching math, but I also use Switched on Schoolhouse, not as their primary source, but as a secondary, and review. Learning about fractions from one source and then having it presented completely different from another source will help ensure their mastery of it. For math in particular, many people only learn one way of approaching a problem. When it is presented differently, a particular component you were sure your child knew may seem completely foreign to him. This is also another way Unit Studies are helpful. The re-introduction of materials from different sources are an invaluable and necessary tool for your homeschool.

ॐ
# Chapter 7

## *Breaking Down Curriculum for Success*

An important aspect of the Workbox System is the philosophy of making the child's materials make sense to them. So often we would like to open a text book, place it in front of the child and simply have them learn. That would be nice. But in reality, it is generally not very interesting for the child, and most often not as successful as we would like. And if you happen to have a special needs child, it may be an impossibility.

There are many common curriculum challenges, regardless of your child's learning style:

*Homeschoolers who spend too much time looking for the **perfect curriculum**.

*Homeschoolers who spend too much time looking for an entire curriculum to meet **one specific need**: like a sticking point in math or grammar.

*Homeschoolers who spend too much money buying every writing curriculum available simply trying to find the one that enables their child to **finally write**.

You can save so much time and money with two simple actions:

1.  Altering or modifying your current curriculum
2.  Writing your own curriculum

Neither of these options may seem attractive to you at the start, but if they seem like they would take too much work, too much time or too much energy, the reality is just the opposite.  They are actually far less of each.  And more importantly—more effective.

I believe that any good, Christian-based curriculum will work with your children, regardless of their learning style.  It may not be the very best, but you bought it for a reason.

Once  you have an understanding of how your child learns and interprets materials, you will easily get the hang of  what your child will most benefit from in changing and altering the materials.

# The following are a few examples of changing existing materials:

**Scientific Speculation Sheet**

Name ___________________________  Date ___________
Experiment Title ____________________________________
Materials Used:

Procedure: (What you will do or what you did)

Hypothesis: (What you think will happen and why)

Results: (What actually happened)

Conclusion: (What you learned)

You have permission to make copies of this form

iv

**Before**

**SCIENCE** **Speculation Sheet**

Title: ___________________________  Date: ___________
Materials Used: _____________________________________
________________________________________________________
________________________________________________________
________________________________________________________

Procedure: (What you will do or what you did) ________________
________________________________________________________
________________________________________________________
________________________________________________________

Hypothesis: (What you think will happen and why) _____________
________________________________________________________
________________________________________________________
________________________________________________________
________________________________________________________

Results: (What actually happened) __________________________
________________________________________________________
________________________________________________________
________________________________________________________

Conclusion: (What you learned) ____________________________
________________________________________________________
________________________________________________________

**After**

This is an example of how a lab sheet was presented in a text book. With just 5 minutes of changes, using Microsoft Publisher, the page on the right is much more inviting to look at, as well as easier for the child to both understand and to write on. The font is larger, there are lines for writing.

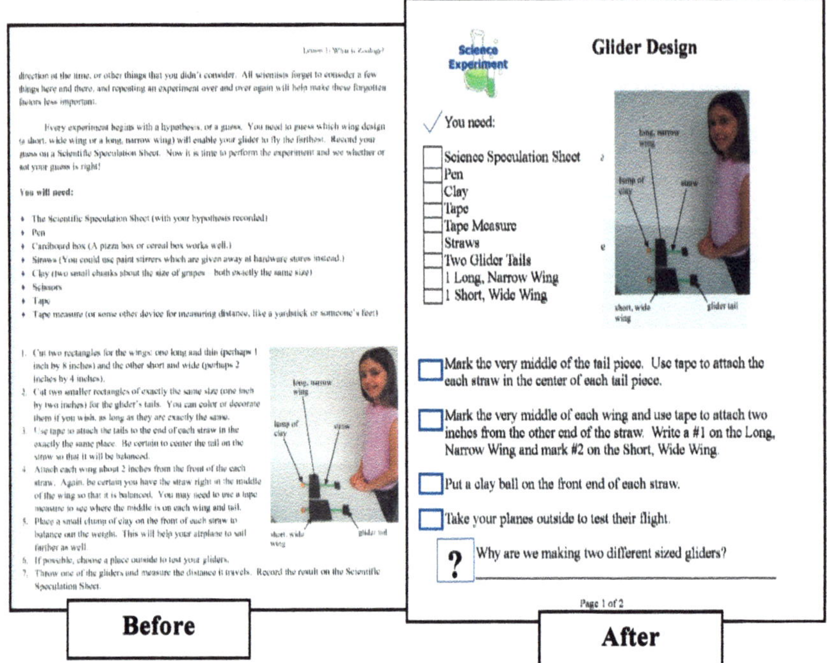

**Before**

**After**

This is an example of a lab that was to be for grades 1 through 6.  I made many changes to enable younger children be able to do the lab themselves, keep moving, understand why they were doing what they were doing, and continually ask themselves questions which allowed for deeper understanding of the material.

So often, science labs are about the teacher telling the child what to do and the child simply acting as a robot, doing what they are told, yet not knowing the reason why.  I made this lab form with check-off points to keep them on track and moving, larger font, and added questions so they would know, or at least wonder why they were doing certain aspects of the experiment.

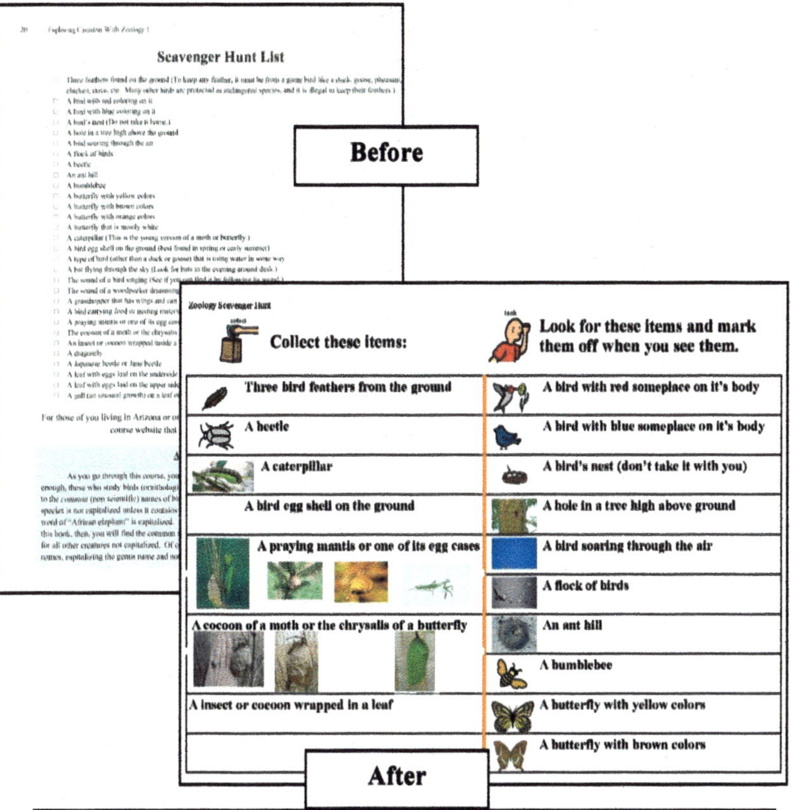



In this instance, the children were to take a scavenger hunt list out to a field trip. The list font was very tiny. Some things were to simply be "seen" and others to be collected. They were not separated on the form.

I re-did the form using mostly Google Images. I designated on the form what was to be collected in their bag and what was to be checked off as seen.

There were also many things that would not have been obvious without a picture, such as a "praying mantis egg case." A picture was necessary to be able to find it. (Don't be intimidated. With practice, this form can quickly and easily be made.)

The following are some samples of making materials for children who needed a concept explained. Often, parents want to find an entire curriculum to teach certain aspects, when it is really easier and more effective to simply make something to explain it or to write your own curriculum.

| Before | Now | Later |
|---|---|---|
|  |  |  |
|  |  |  |
|  |  |  |
|  |  |  |
|  |  |  |
|  |  |  |
|  |  |  |
|  |  |  |
|  |  |  |
|  |  |  |

| today | yesterday | tomorrow |
|---|---|---|
| I am going there. | I went there. | I am here. |
| She left. | She is leaving. | She is going to leave. |
| The dog barked | The dog is barking. | The dog will bark when the mailman comes. |
| The sun came up. | The sun is up. | The sun will go down. |
| I am hungry. | I will eat. | I already ate lunch. |
| I was dirty. | I am taking a shower. | I am clean. |
| We are going to the movies. | This movie is funny. | Yesterday we went to the funny movie. |
| November | October | December |
| morning | daytime | evening |

This is an example of an issue a child had with grammar tense. The mom was interested in a "curriculum" to address the problem. She didn't need a new curriculum, just a separate activity addressing the problem. Here, the child was to cut out the sentences and place them in the correct column.

Often, your children simply need more practice and repetition. Though you may be certain he should understand the material by now...he just doesn't.  For example, time and money can take some children a very long time to master.  Place a bingo card in their Workbox, with the magnetic bingo chips (added measure of fun), and all the matching cards needed to fill the bingo cards.  Call out each one and by the end, all the spaces are filled.  You are not really playing a true bingo game, but doing it this way will work on logic, by using the process of elimination if he truly doesn't know the answer, as well as working on the true math of it.  It is also more fun to work on a hard subject while he is getting to play a game with mom.

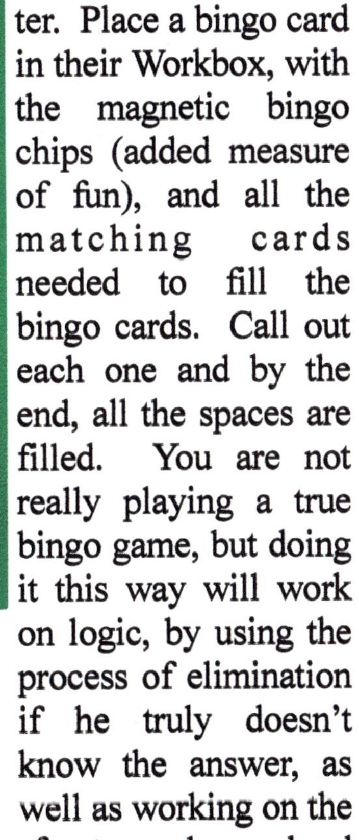

Another very simple approach is to make sure each Workbox is appropriate for their ability and attention span. Some children may need a math sheet cut in half, or even enlarged on your printer. Then place half of the math sheet in one Workbox and the other half several Workboxes later. That way, the work is still done, but doesn't seem quite so overwhelming. This is also a great option for reading. If the child is to read 20 pages of his reader. Place the book and a yellow sticky instructing him to read the first 10 pages in Box 2 and then a yellow sticky by itself in Box 7 instructing him to get the book again and read the next 10 pages.

One final aspect of breaking down curriculum I would like you to be consistently aware of is that you are careful not to have the child working on too many skills at one time. Very often, if a child is being behavioral during school, it is a result of the work either not making sense to him or being too difficult because he is being forced to work on too many skills at one time. This is another area where it can be difficult to discern simply because you know the material, and it seems quite easy to you. Take a look at the work closely. Is he having to read, and write, and compose and calculate?....the list could go on without your realizing all that is involved. You can still give the same work and assignment, yet take some aspect of a too difficult skill out of it. Perhaps you provide labels with answers so that he doesn't have to write. He still would need to select the correct answer. Or maybe he can type his answers instead of writing. I allow my son to use a word prediction program when he is writing. That way, the skills of spelling and, to some extent, composing are greatly relieved. He is still the one writing the story and getting the words onto paper. See Chapter 12 for word prediction software.

ꙮ
# Chapter 8

## *Life Skill Foundations*

There are three foundations that I believe are very important to build upon in your homeschool from the very beginning. Some people naturally work on these, but perhaps not throughout the child's education. Elementary ages are not the only age to work on basics. Compared to the rest of their lives, the high school years are still foundational years.

## Typing

One such foundation that I think parents believe will just fall into place is typing. Typing correctly is more important than you might think. And because children are using computers at very young ages, I recommend teaching the correct way to type at a young age. That way the bad habits may be minimized and the benefits of proper typing will be of great help throughout their entire lives. I have a developed a typing system in which even young children will learn to type correctly. It involves placing a template of a keyboard on the wall in front of them and covering their hands (yourself) with either a large piece of construction paper or a placemat.  In the very beginning, they should never look at their fingers or at what they have typed.

If they need to know where a key is, they look up at the keyboard template. I also think it is best to make a Typing Center and for the children to learn on an actual typewriter.  Though typewriters are scarce these days, it is well worth the (lifetime) investment in your child.  A computer, while it will work, has too many distractions. Also, children may be too con-cerned with accuracy (which promotes looking at their fingers) to progress well enough.

For the Typing Center, I keep a separate desk area with the appropriate size of desk  and chair and I have set up a Word file with pages printed in large font. I have logically set up each practice page according to home row and adding keys over time. Most children will learn to proficiently type in a couple of months—especially if the typing center is put on their Workbox Schedule daily.

Sample typing center. Initially hold a large piece of construction paper over their hands. Only allow the child to look at the colorful template above the typewriter—not their hands, not the keyboard.

It does take discipline on your part to stick by them and never let them look at their fingers, make sure they have the proper posture and technique, and are using the correct fingers for the correct keys. This is a "Work with Mom," Work-box initially,  but children learn very quickly and once they learn these for each key, they will be flying in no time.

After comfortably learning all the keys and typing without looking at their fingers, they may then play the computer typing programs.  My particular favorite is Typer Shark.  It is excellent, next level, practice once they have learned all the keys.

Though there are many programs made for the computer to teach our children to type, they will not achieve the skill and accuracy with these distracting programs.

## Sequencing Skills

Sequencing skills are another important foundation we should be teaching our children from the very beginning.  I believe that we have so many environmental factors today chipping away at our sequencing skills.  Sequencing is involved in everything we learn and everything we do.  And there seems to be a rash of children who are lacking this developmental level.  I am suspicious of television and computer/ video games being a culprit in this decline.

Sequencing skills are important in learning to potty train, learning how to read and write, learning to drive a car, as well as for keeping themselves organized enough to graduate from college. It truly is a lifelong foundational skill and it is worth working on throughout life.

One of the values in starting the Workbox System with toddlers is that it naturally begins teaching sequencing. From following the schedule strip to doing their Workboxes from left to right and top to bottom, the Workbox System will help them work on sequencing from the beginning. This is such strong training for sequencing that it will actually set the stage for learning to read and write. Children do not naturally move left to right and top to bottom. Left to their own, they will move in any order that comes to mind.

Throughout their homeschool education, it is a good idea to provide many materials, toys and curriculum to work on sequencing. It will serve them well throughout their lives.

## Discipline

The third foundational life skill is discipline. I have gone over discipline in another chapter, but it is very important. In our homeschools, we can take the time that is not afforded in teaching the masses. And the child who learns the skill of self discipline early in life will be very well served by it throughout their lives.

The Workbox System naturally works on discipline when we use the system correctly. It is never OK for them not to finish their Workboxes. And this is never more true and important than in the very beginning of your incorporating this system into your homeschool. Your expectations and tone can set the stage for continued success when you are strict in the beginning. The children are never to go out of order of the schedule strip, they are to finish all work and finish it well. The more consistent you are in following through with this system as well as in your consistency to have school every scheduled day, you will be setting an important example in discipline.

The discipline to do chores every day, to have school and put in a full effort every day, to run on the treadmill every day...all builds a life skill and a habit of discipline.

I believe these three foundations: typing, sequencing and discipline are equally as important as the academics you teach in your school.

ॐ

## Chapter 9

## *Discipline and the Workbox System*

Discipline is something that is important to me on many levels, but I am not simply referring to your child's outward behavior. I mean their heart and I also mean **your** effort. You can lead a horse to water, but you can't make him drink. Though you can either entice him to drink, or you can make him miserable until he does drink. While I certainly end up using both techniques at times, it's a lot more enjoyable all around to entice.

Your child may not like working on multiplication, but a simple center project will seem incredibly fun and nothing like work. And by using his mind, hands, interests, and emotions, suddenly multiplication is not only fun, but is easier to learn. And before you know it, the child that was a behavior problem when it came to math is now looking forward to math. Where was the discipline? The discipline was in you to look at what he was interested in vs. what he was not interested in and to look at what was not previously getting through to him. The discipline was in your being willing to problem solve and come up with a solution. It's not his job to learn how to learn, it's your job to teach in a way that he will learn. It takes discipline to treat homeschooling as a full time job that you are not only committed to, but responsible for.

I am **not** interested in helping homeschoolers figure out how they can do their laundry, cooking and cleaning while homeschooling their children. I am **very** interested in getting homeschoolers to focus on homeschooling—period. Isn't that what you want your children to do?

> *"It's not his job to learn how to learn, it's your job to teach in a way he will learn."*

Accordingly, discipline issues in homeschooling are greatly diminished when you use the Workbox System with a thought process of problem solving, breaking down curriculum and being in tune with your child. Most focus issues and whining during the school day are not about your child being bad. They are about the way the work is set before them. The more the work makes sense to them, the easier it will be for them to learn and you will all benefit from a more positive day.

It is important to break down a child's work into the smallest and yet largest amount he can handle.

We often do not realize how many skills we are asking them to work on at one time. The material is so familiar to us, that it's hard for us to realize the work involved in starting from scratch on a particular subject.

It is a good idea to look at every Workbox you give them with fresh eyes, paying close attention to the number of skills that will be necessary to complete the work. Math is never just math. It's often reading, following directions, writing, and sequencing. If your child has matured to a level to handle all these skills at one time, then simply learning the math portion will be easier. However, if he has difficulty with any or all of these skills, then the math part will be insurmountable on top of trying to utilize the other skills he has not mastered, all at the same time.

The better you know your child's mind, the more success you will have in the presentation of his work. If writing is the stumbling block, and that is not the primary subject for that Workbox, then allow for an alternative for the writing component. I am a huge fan of the label printer. It is small, economical and can be used countless ways in homeschooling. I will give you more ideas in Chapter 12, but by printing out words, answers and even sentences onto labels, you can take that skill effort out of that Workbox so that your child can focus on the primary subject.

If your child appears to have behavior problems with reading, there is surely a reason behind it. Laziness is not always the reason—in fact it rarely is. Often it has more to do with sequencing issues or even the ability to sit still for any period of time. If the child is older, it may be difficult for him to sequence the characters and events. By simply providing a sheet of paper (with "Name" and "What they Did" on top of the paper) to list each character name and the event, in conjunction with having them read only a few pages at a time may be the answer. Add to that a quick question and answer sheet or, even more fun, a homemade test with Microsoft Word*. They may find the structure of the listings and the questions to be helpful with their comprehension. Then their success with these will build an interest in reading.

If the child is younger, the sequencing issue may be with each individual word formation, the size of the print or the length of the reading. Again, I would find a way to break the material down into smaller pieces or organize the reading into a visually structured way to increase success. I find that it is much

*See Resources

easier for children to learn to read after they have mastered approximately 1000 sight words. Without first having a good number of sight words, it is difficult to present the concept of phonics or its purpose. Again, we cannot assume they will know how to learn or that the concept of reading will make sense to them. We must first teach them how to learn. And with a foundation of very simple kindergarten type sight words, most children will then be ready for phonics and decoding. Having the foundation of the sight words will take away the overwhelming skill of having to decode every single word in the sentence. Most of those early sight words they can then skim over easily when reading and they are only working on the skill of phonics for the much more involved words. This will take much of the labor out of learning to read and subsequently give them a greater ability to sit still and hang in there.

# Chapter 10

## *Problem Solving and Specializing your Child's Homeschooling*

There are a few people out there with a child or perhaps two that naturally loves to learn, is a self-starter, and is creatively teaching themselves. I have heard of such children, but I've never seen one in action. And if they do exist, their siblings are not so. If you are blessed to have such a child, great, he or she will help you to get the Workbox System in place. They are probably   organized and motivated and will surely be a great help.

The rest of you (us) will address our children who have attitude challenges, learning disabilities and sticking points in their education. These are the areas we need to problem solve. This is my specialty. I love it. But paramount to problem solving, you must know your child—how he thinks, what he understands and what he doesn't understand. It's very easy to learn what he doesn't understand. But when you put it together with what he does understand you can present the material differently—aimed at his way of thinking.

Your teaching, and your entire school day is observing your child and what he has learned and can learn. It's also changing, sometimes on the fly, the way material is presented because it didn't make sense to him. The way material is presented in a text can be very difficult to understand. But if you break the material up into pieces, and show (often physically or hands-on) examples of what the author is talking about, it will be much easier to learn. For example:

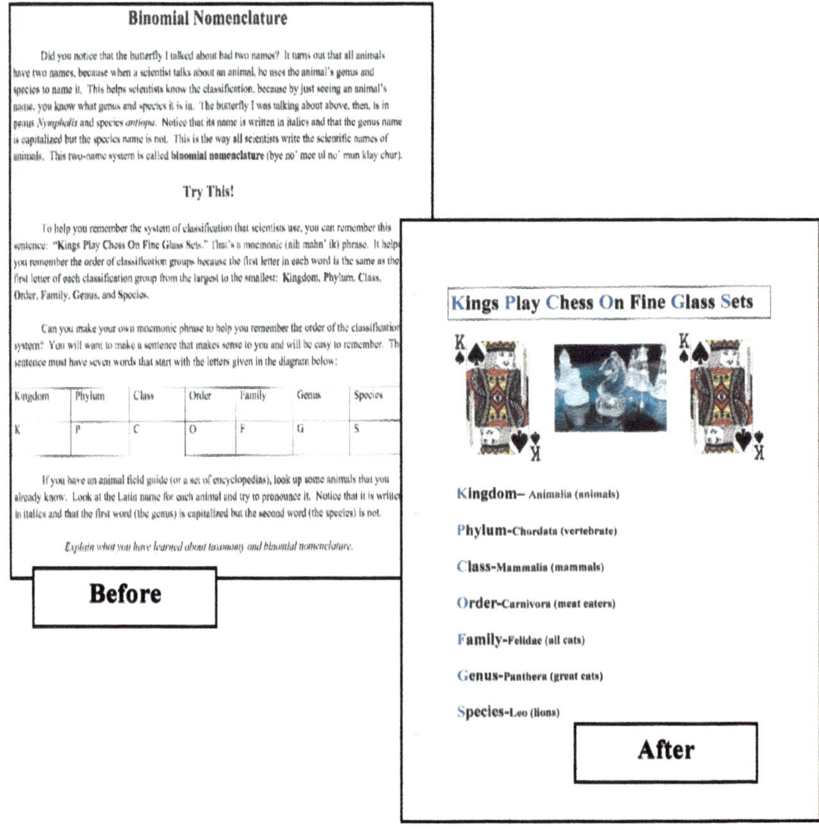

Changing this material took little effort but created an environment for precious great gain. You can go through this material as it is, but it may mean nothing the next day.

Once children are trained on the Workbox System, you will find that any bad behavior during school is usually a result of the material being too hard or not making sense to them. Often when the materials are simply broken into small pieces over more than one Workbox, the behavior goes away. If it doesn't, that is when you need to reassess the material:

* Do you need to break it up into
   smaller pieces?
* Do you need to present it totally
   differently?
* Do you need to make it more
   tactile or more visual?
* Do you  need to change the
   vocabulary or the way it is
   described in the instructions?
* Do you need to add in more
   repetition?
* Do you need to put it away
   and bring it out again in 6 months,
   a year or two years when they
   are better able to understand it?

I have had many pieces of curriculum that I purchased only to find that I bought it a year or two ahead of when my child was ready for it.

☙✿❧

# Chapter 11

## *Family Dynamics and Homeschooling*

### *Very Large Families*

The Workbox System works very well for large families. You can come together for group learning when it is appropriate, keep your children working independently, and also incorporate small children into your homeschool, keeping them appropriately busy while giving them a sense of inclusion with the big kids. With everyone doing the Workbox System, there are less distractions and less re-acclamation for you as you bounce between students for one-on-one instruction. When you gather together for family learning, it so easy for everyone to then get back to their own independent learning instantaneously and without confusion.

The Workbox System also allows a very structured way for older students to help younger students. Without structure, a younger child may not have the ability to learn from an older child. For the older child, the structure allows them to confidently work with young ones and gives them a real sense of helpfulness and accomplishment. This is an invaluable family relationship building tool.

Children who are very close in age can help each other by utilizing one child's strengths to help another's weakness in the same area. Often the best way to learn is to teach. It makes for a great sibling relationship when children can share their strengths in helping one another. Everyone benefits from the unique strengths of each child. It also helps children to feel appreciated as they work together.

### *Very Young Families*

Very young children thrive on structure. Providing structure in the form of their physical environment as well as the structuring of their schedule will help tremendously. Most children have an intense need to know what is next, when is lunch, what is their day, what is tomorrow…it goes on. Some children may thrive on the unknown, but most will feel better, behave better and learn better on a schedule.

A schedule for behavior, a schedule for expectations, and a schedule for school will help your children to better meet your expectations and help your home run more smoothly. It is not as much effort on your part as you may think, and the benefits will be phenomenal.

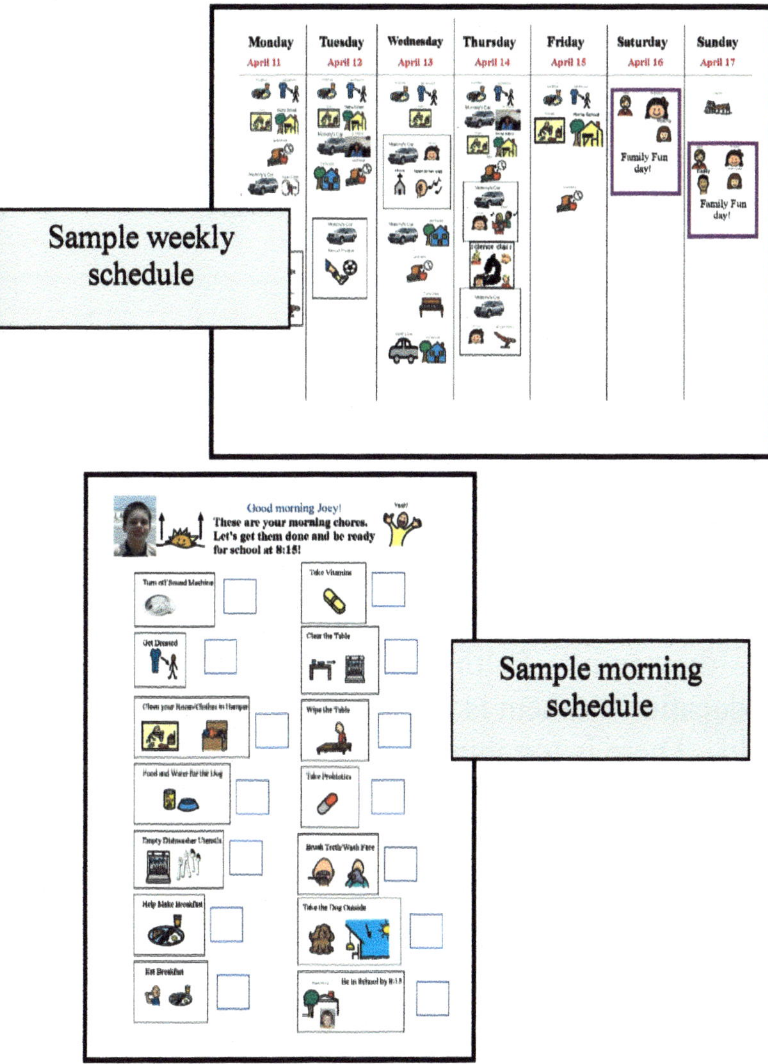

Sample weekly schedule

Sample morning schedule

## *High Schoolers*

This is where I would like to make my plea.  I talk to so many homeschoolers of High Schoolers with frustration issues.  Most of those frustrations may be alleviated by the Workbox System.  Very often the issues are related to two things:

1. Some parents are expecting High Schoolers to learn completely on their own and be  responsible for their own education
2. Attitude

While it's true that every homeschool will be different and every parent gets to have their say, I truly believe this theory of complete independence in high school is a big mistake.  While these children may look like adults and want to be adults—they aren't.  Putting the responsibility for their education on them is too much for a 15 to 18 year old.  There is too much going on in their development, too many temptations and too many things competing for their time.  If left to their own devices, school is not going to be their first priority—even if they want it to be.  It is too easy to think they have things under control, to think they will get to their work "when the time is right," and to think they can handle it. Not to mention those children who know they can't handle it.

We are their parents and their teachers. The teaching should not end because they are in High School. There are plenty of responsible children out there. That is great, let them be independent with special projects and subjects. But we should be teaching, supervising and checking up on all their work all the way through graduation. It's been said that people do what you inspect, not what you expect. It's hard enough for a responsible adult to do the things they need to do, much less to expect a child to do it.

Using the Workbox System for High Schoolers will make teaching them and inspecting their work all the easier. Sometimes a High School parent's initial reaction to the Workbox System is that it seems too immature for a High Schooler. But with all the competition that High Schoolers have for their time and focus, the Workbox System is just what they need.

Changing from the Workboxes to file folders is not the answer. It is far too easy for a file folder to be moved from one place to another and never be opened. The child never opens it to do their work and the parent never opens it to check and see if the work has been done. Business file folders always seem like a more mature way to use the Workbox System theory, but it is at least 60% less effective. There really is no good reason to give up on the Workboxes.

## *Preschoolers*

Here is the other end of the spectrum. The larger the family, the more these little people are left to their own devices. Younger children, especially in large families do tend to develop a certain independence that child #1 and #2 didn't seem to develop, but that's not necessarily a good thing. And the homeschoolers who choose to do school when the little ones are napping are, I believe, cheating the older children out of a good deal of educational opportunities.

> *"Some children may thrive on the unknown, but most will feel better, behave better and learn better on a schedule."*

You really can incorporate very young children in school. I started both my children in the classroom with the Workbox System at 18 months old and it really is very easy. Why should those little ones be banished to a separate room, or worse yet, to TV, when all they want is to be with the rest of the family? You can take advantage of that natural ability for independence and get their education off to the right start.

Their Workboxes will contain either toys, fine motor skill objects, or life skills learning. The important thing to remember is that, like your school aged children, the work in their Workboxes must be obvious as to what needs to be done. Their work must have a beginning, middle and obvious end. If you put play dough in the Workbox, they won't know how long to play with it. If you put beads and a string, they will know they are done when all the beads are on the string. If you have an open ended toy in their Workbox, then they will need some form of a cue to know how long to play with it before going on to the next Workbox. For young children, much of their work will be "Work with Mom" when each type of work is initially introduced since they would not be able to read instructions.

A preschooler should have just as much right to have training and "Work with Mom" Workboxes as anyone else in the family. If you spend a day really training your preschooler on the Workbox System, you will quite literally have school obedience with them for life. They will always know and never question that this is school, to proceed until all their work is done and this is where they work.

There are free resources abounding over the Internet for preschool education. Simply Google "free preschool curriculum," and you will have enough free materials to last forever.

One particular preschool resource I would like to give special mention to is the <u>The Best of Mailbox Learning Centers Preschool/Kindergarten</u>. The projects in this book are invaluable for the development of your child at this age.

The Workbox System is also a wonderful tool for teaching life skills to preschoolers. My children learned how to dress themselves, tie their shoes, sort and organize, and even set the table by using this system when they were so very young. For example, three of the Workboxes lined up on their bed provide the structure they need to keep moving and get themselves dressed. A row of Workboxes lined up on the coffee table will be just the thing to keep your toddler appropriately busy while you make dinner. The opportunities and the advantages are limitless.

### *Your Special Needs Child*

Many to most people feel their children all have a special need of one form or another, but the truly special needs child will benefit the most from the Workbox System. I have worked with so many families whose child had quite literally never learned anything academic until the Workbox System. There are many children that we will never be able to open a textbook for or use a "regular" curriculum. They wouldn't be able to decipher it—even with our help.

> *"So many special needs children can learn anything, yet must be taught everything."*

I am rather shocked at the number of families I have met that homeschool their "typical" children and send their special needs child to public school. Special needs children should be the greatest target of all for homeschooling. These children need the specialized academic attention they will never receive in public school. So many special needs children can learn anything, yet must be taught everything. They don't magically absorb information, or formulate learning processes on their own. Perhaps the simplest of ideas must be specifically taught. Yet everything they are taught will ultimately help in one way or another. It is never a waste to learn anything. And it's certainly worth the effort for us to teach them.

Any situation that we come into in life is made more successful with familiarity. For a special needs child, the more knowledge, experience and information we can provide them, the better they can handle the "world." We must plan for the times they are not with us. Whether it's an outing, a group event or when we pass away before them, they will be on their own in some way. We can never over-prepare them for independence. The more they learn and experience in a structured way, the better they will handle the unstructured.

I believe there are three components to approaching educating and raising our special needs children. Those three components are:

1. Teaching them how to Learn and Think
2. Teaching them Life Skills
3. Teaching Academics

These components should be taught primarily I in that order, however, all three will need to be taught on a continuum. While typical children may simply absorb learning skills and life skills,

these must be isolated and taught in and of themselves to many special needs children.  Teaching
them how to Learn and Think first, will take a lot
of frustration out of your relationship and
homeschooling and ultimately make both of you
feel much more successful.  This first component
may take much longer than you wish, but will be
well worth it.

### *Teaching your special needs child how to learn*

Many of us are blessed to be able to just somehow know how our child thinks and learns.  The
rest of us must work with trial and error much of
the time.  It is important to start with the assump-
tion that they must be taught the smallest detail.
For example, if your child is 5 and you would like
him to read, presenting him with the alphabet is
not the starting point.  He must first be able to understand some important underlying points that
though many children just absorb, your child may
need to be taught.

Learning to sit still in a chair is more important
than you might think.  Learning to be quiet without speaking every thought that comes to his
mind is important.  Understanding that the characters written on the page actually mean some-

thing—telling them that they are going to read doesn't mean a thing to some children and they have no idea what you are talking about—nor do they care.

Moving your special needs child into the world of reading is huge.  Whether your child is 3 or 15, learning to read will open up a whole new world of educational opportunities.  Our society reads and without that skill, your child will be severely limited.

Just as with preschoolers, I don't believe your special needs child will be able to grasp phonics until they have almost 2000 sight words.  The way I like to get them started is not to present simply written sight words, but to present pictures with the words written under the picture.  I also like to use desktop publishing to make up books for the child, pertaining to his or her interest, using the pictures paired with the words.  I like to read these books to them over and over and as they memorize the book, take away the picture and leave the printed word.  This creates a meaningful way for them to grasp reading and sight words at the same time.  This can be an extremely rewarding activity for you to make, because many children who have not learned to read before will learn to read these homemade books rather

make more and more new books incorporating the memorized words from the old books. Often you will not need the picture for the words in a new book because they learned it so well in the past book.

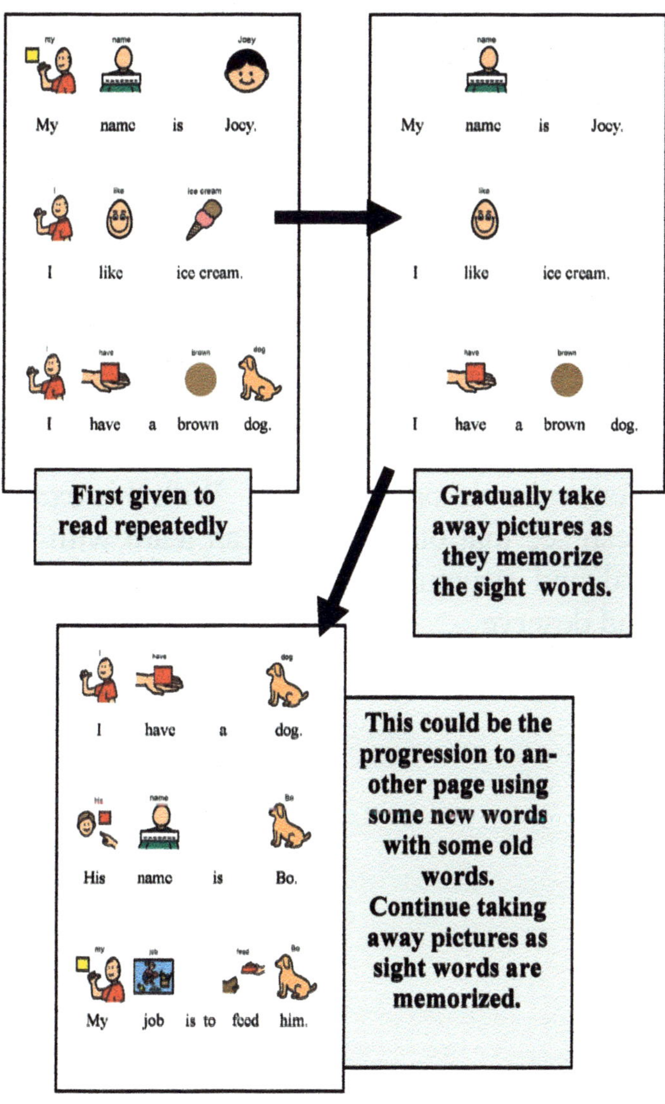

The point of making these homemade books, as opposed to using any little young reader you may buy off the shelf, is that this is of much higher interest to your child, and you are able to manipulate the pictures and words much easier to promote memorizing the sight words which will lead to an easier approach to phonics.

As I stated previously, your special needs child must be taught **how** to learn. Breaking down reading and using a lot of repetition, as shown above is just one example of how your special needs child can learn to learn and progress at his pace. It has been my experience that many special needs children are not being taught to read and as a result are excluded from many other academic opportunities. With this example, you can see that our children can learn with the specialized and structured individual teaching they require and deserve.

ᘏᘎᘋ
# Chapter 12

## *Tips, Tricks and Problem Solving*

### *Tips and Tricks*

Adding a rich assortment of the following materials will make all the difference in your homeschool. You may think of many of these items as being a part of a professional office, school or business—guess what, you are all of these.

The following list of items may seem expensive or extravagant, but over the life of your school, the benefits of this equipment and these materials will prove to be essential. You may check the Resources section for where to find these items.

**Laminator**– I recommend a "hot" laminator, as well as one able to accept items 13" or larger. Everything looks better when it's laminated, lasts longer and is more versatile. You can then use Velcro and dry erase markers on the materials. Velcro will not stick to "cold" laminator lamination.

**Binding Machine**–A comb binding machine

should do the trick.  There are several benefits to having a binding machine—putting together Unit Studies, making your own books, putting together worksheets (if you put three worksheets in a Workbox, it seems overwhelming, but if they are bound, they won't). It's convenient to cut bindings off books, putting them back together with the binding machine.

**Label Printer**-These very small printers are thermal (no ink needed) and provide limitless uses. Great to relieve handwriting stress by providing information on labels, making flashcards, organizing, lapbooking, and the list goes on.

**Velcro**-Again, limitless uses. Essential for putting together the Workbox System, as well as file folder activities, posters, centers and more.

**High Quality Printer**-Options such as paper feed,  scanning, double-sided printing (saves an incredible amount of paper), and a large paper tray will prove beneficial.  Many of your activities will be much easier to assemble, such as file folder activities, centers and Unit Studies when you have higher quality equipment.  And the better the printer, the easier it is to use a refill, or **continuous fill ink system,** which can make your printing costs next to nothing—well outweighing the cost of a more expensive printer.

**Board Games**-I believe if all we ever did was play board games, our children would learn everything they needed to know and be able to graduate from High School. There is an incredibly rich array of board games to develop your children in areas such as logic, sequencing, memory skills, and all areas of academics. Plus, board games are a great family relationship activity.

**Audio Books**-Audio Books are often free at your local library, and can be invaluable to the reluctant reader, the struggling reader, a dyslexic child, very young children,  as well as a great option for school centers.

**Word Prediction Software**-Certainly not used by mainstream schools or homeschools, but more beneficial than you may think. This software works such that when you type a letter, the most popular words in the English language pop up in a box, as you continue to type a word, the most popular words following that word pop up. This can save a lot of time and frustration for children with difficulty in spelling and composition. It will give an invaluable amount of support and confidence to many children who would not normally want to write or even email.

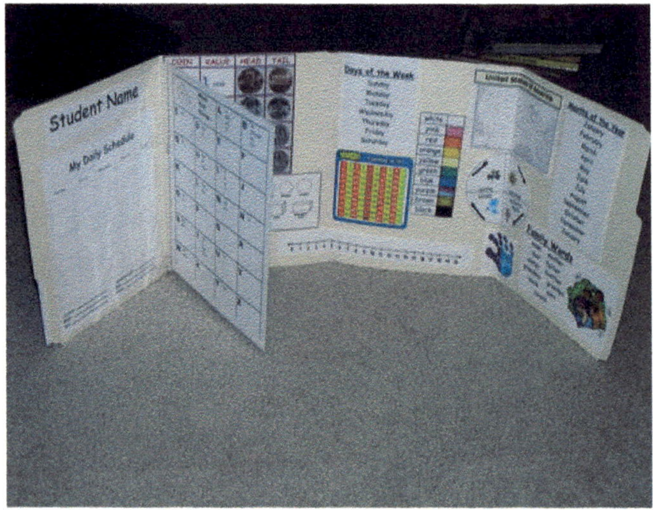

**Mini-Office-**These are very helpful, convenient references catered specially to your child.  I suggest making these up for the things your child must refer to often, or has the most trouble  remembering.  The longer the information is in front of them, the greater the chance they will memorize it.  These can be utilized from pre-school through high school.  Preschool might cover a calendar, days of the week and colors, while a high schooler's may cover equations from math, physics or chemistry as well as grammar and writing points of reference.

## *Problem Solving*

When I speak to homeschooling groups, I always bring a lot of my "homemade" materials.  There is nothing like a visual to get a point across.  This is true for adults and children alike.  Most of these visual examples I have made are the result of  problems in homeschooling that a parent has presented me with.  And most problems are considered just that due to a child's behavior.  Most of the undesirable school behaviors are due to a problem with how their work is presented to them.

Most homeschoolers love seeing all the materials I make, and  claim that I must be creative.  As I stated in an earlier chapter, I am not creative.  I make these materials and projects  based on problems and issues children have.  When I look at a problem a child is having, it is almost always about the work being too overwhelming in some way.  Many parents' gut reaction is that it is laziness in the child.  But I find that most solutions lie in taking a close look at the problem and discerning the real issues.  Generally approaching the same work in one of three ways will greatly alleviate the problem.

1. Make the material more hands-on.

2. Make up materials to create more repetition.

3. Make sure that there are not too many emergent skills (skills they have not yet mastered) required to complete the work.

I truly find that one of these three is either the culprit or is needed to correct the problem. It is never a waste of effort to the make the work more hands-on.

## *More Hands-on Materials*

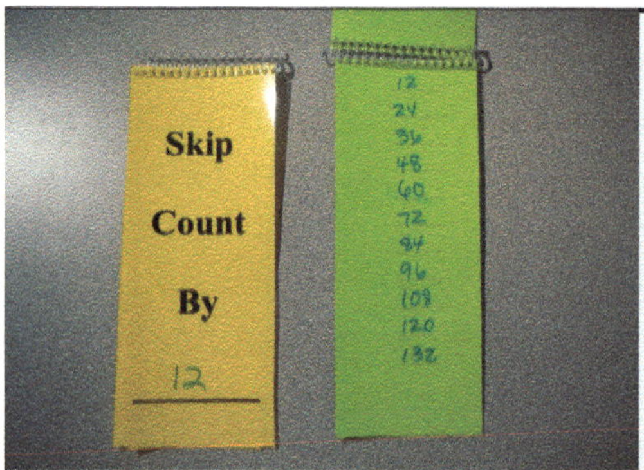


In this case, I wanted more skip counting practice, as well as a greater understanding of multiplication. I didn't want my children to memorize the multiplication table. This activity was something to look forward to in a Workbox, made the concept very hands-on and was a very good repetition activity for years. I would simply slip about three of these in a Workbox. It's also good mental math.

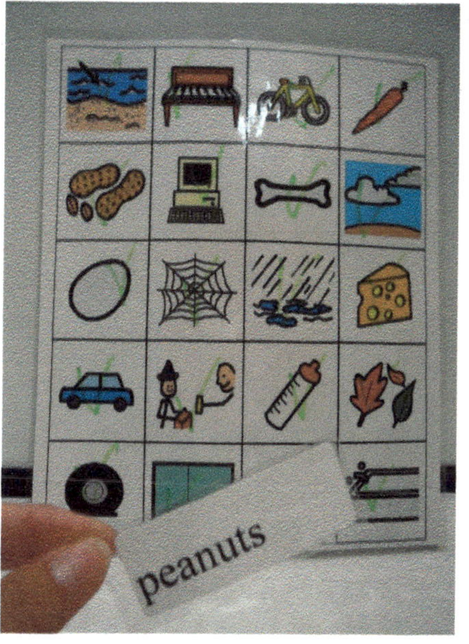



This was for a non-verbal child that I wanted to be sure truly understood the words he was reading. I printed out his vocabulary words and made up a picture grid for each word and laminated it. As I showed the words, he would use a dry-erase marker and mark them off. I could then be sure he was reading.

This child had difficulty with greater than and less than. I first gave this "story" explaining that the alligator wants to eat the "greater" amount of food. Then I copied the alligator, made him two-sided for Greater Than and Less Than and laminated it. The Alligator was reversible, allowing the child to pick the correct answer and then write it on the page. It finally made sense to this child.

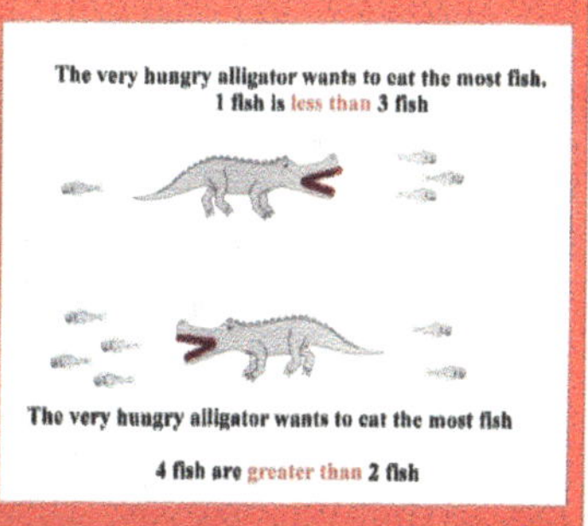

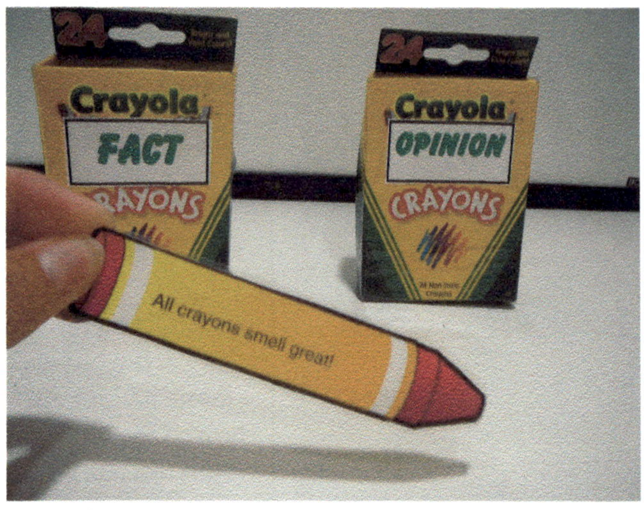



I find a lot of children have difficulty discerning fact vs. opinion.  This was a great hands-on activity to work on this skill.  Hands on is so often more effective than paper and pencil.

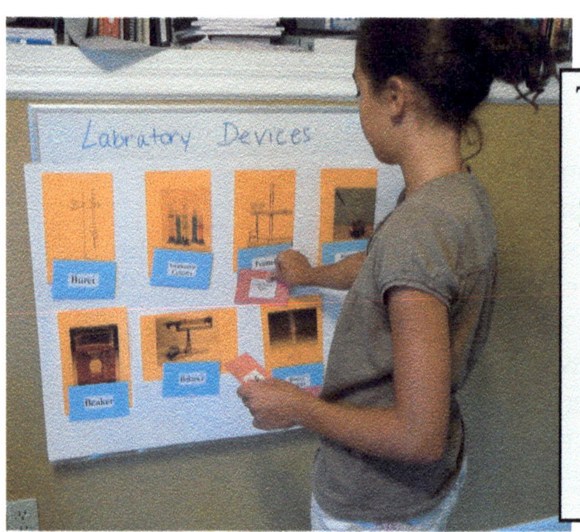



This was a very quick and simple way of introducing laboratory equipment before using it.  It covered the name of each piece of equipment as well as the definition.
This was not fancy, but it was hands-on.

Each of these previous examples are both hands-on, and may be continued to be used for review and repetition. You will need to continually assess, from their work output, level of frustration, and ability to complete the work independently, where there is a need to alter or add to their curriculum.

## *Social Stories*

Social Stories are an important tool for communicating with all children, but they are especially helpful to special needs children. I find that few people are familiar with Social Stories, but when I introduce them for their children, the stories have been very successful in helping children understand discipline, social interaction, expectations, and peer interactions. For example, one subject that has been particularly helpful for several children have been the death of a family member. Other topics have included obsessive/perfectionism issues, temper management, and appropriate social behavior. But these stories can be very helpful for all children and a wide array of circumstances.

This is an example that can be posted in a restroom to help children move through the steps of using the restroom. Often, too much talking to them can confuse them. But the visual may be just what they need.

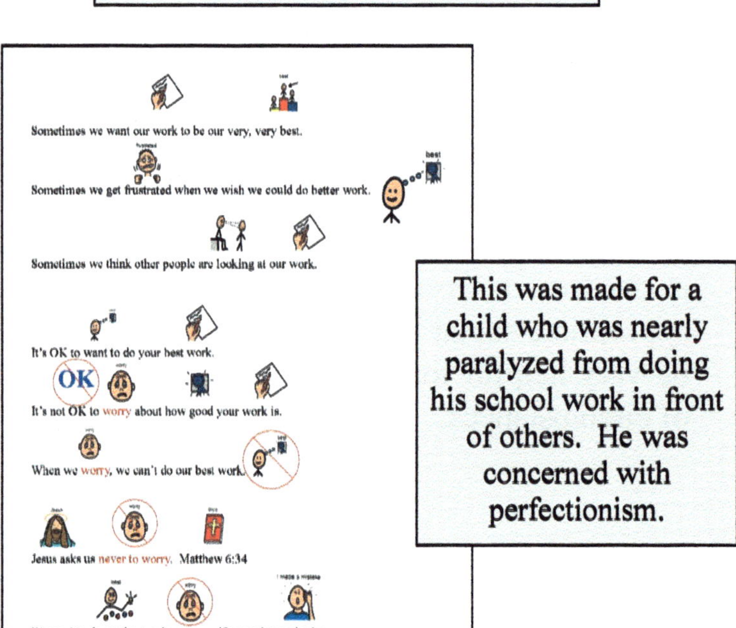

This was made for a child who was nearly paralyzed from doing his school work in front of others. He was concerned with perfectionism.

## ❧ Resources

The following is a list of resources, though my website will continue to be updated with new resource information.

### *Computer Resources*

Tutorial for making interactive forms and tests in Microsoft Word:
> **www.education-world.com/a_tech/ techtorial/techtorial020.shtml**

My favorite desktop publishing program:
> Microsoft Publisher

Favorite Free Program:
> Open Office

This program duplicates all the Microsoft Office Products

Picture programs for making schedules, social stories, projects like altering curriculum:

Google Images:  these are free—simply go to the normal Google search and click on "Images" instead of "Web."

Boardmaker:  This is not free ($400), but is a

wonderful investment if you have young children or special needs children.

Typing: Typer Shark. Available from several sources, but very easily downloaded from Yahoo Games.

Word Prediction: My favorite is Word Q. You may download a free 30 day trial from:
**www.wordq.com/**

Great place to buy many computer programs:
**www.academicsuperstore.com**
Many programs you must provide proof of homeschooling/teacher (I sent a copy of my Sonlight Curriculum purchase order). The savings can be substantial. Microsoft Office 2007 is approximately $300 in stores and only $99 at Academic Superstore.

Downloadable File Folder Activities and Centers:
**www.teacherfilebox.com**
More information on File Folder and Center sources is on the next page, but this source has a monthly membership fee of $10 and you have hundreds of options from Evan Moor to print and use.

Velcro: My favorite source for 1/2" coins.
**www.feinersupply.com**

# File Folder and Center Project Sources:
## www.teacherfilebox.com

## The Best of Mailbox Learning Centers
These come in several grade levels:
Preschool through 6th Grade

## Evan Moor Publications:
They have many excellent options:

Two examples
of their many
books.
They are all
worthwhile.

This series has books for Math, Literacy and
Science, ranging from Kindergarten through
6th Grade.  The 6th Grade centers could still be
used for review through middle school.
Nearly all of their projects are available
through membership to
www.teacherfilebox.com

## Carson-Dellosa Publications for File Folders:

> This series is less expensive, but requires more work on your part. These come black/white, and are more work to put together.

There are more versions and publishers of file folder activities and centers, these were just an example. You can usually find any/all of them on Ebay for a good price.

Laminator:  I love my GBC 4250.  This is a commercial size laminator (will laminate up to 25").  These are large, but well worth the investment and size. They are very expensive new, but can be purchased very reasonably on Ebay ($100 to $200).  You may also get great deals on smaller laminators on Ebay. As mentioned earlier, I recommend at least a 13" heat laminator which you should be able to find one for less than $65.

Lamination Film:
### www.oregonlam.com
This is the best place to buy whether you are buying the "pockets" as for smaller laminators or

the film rolls for the larger laminators.

## Storage Ideas

Poster storage works very well in the tri-fold display boards from AC Moore or Michaels.  They will hold many posters and store nicely (flat) many places easily.  There are also very nice cardboard boxes made just for storing posters at teacher supply stores, but these do cost a little more—yet hold a lot more.

Business Folder Plastic Totes work very well for storing File Folders and Centers.

## Creating Wall Space for Posters
Home Depot or Lowes have a product created for shower surrounds.  It is very inexpensive, approximately $9 for a 9' x 7' sheet.  These sheets are also equivalent to dry erase boards.

Their uses abound. I buy them and have my husband cut them into sizes more convenient for the classroom. I hang some above each child's desk for writing notes/information and teaching, and some I use as a "portable wall" for hanging posters—simply place a couple pieces of Velcro across the top. Mine is about 4' x 4'. The back is reinforced with 1" x 1" wood strips to give it more support. This also functions nicely as an extra large table top for wrapping presents, working on large projects, or playing large games like dominos.

Place Velcro across the top to hang posters.

Reinforced back of the white board.

# *Notes*

# *Notes*

# Notes

# *Notes*